A FEW
STEPS
AWAY
FROM
VICTORY

Choosing to Walk in Divine Purpose

DESOLYN L. HICKS

A Few Steps Away from Victory
Choosing to Walk into Divine Purpose
By Desolyn L. Hicks

ISBN: 978-0-692-15094-8

Copyright © 2018. All rights reserved
Published by Faithcures
P.O. Box 136
Sugar Land, TX 77487

www.faithcures.com

DEDICATION

I dedicate this book to my first and true love, God!

Secondly, I dedicate this book to women
that have been hurt deeply by someone
that you trusted wholeheartedly.

ACKNOWLEDGMENTS

My beloved and amazing two daughters, for
inspiring me to love unconditionally and be grateful
for each day of God's new mercies and grace.

My dear mom, for teaching me about Jesus and giving
me so much wisdom about life. Beloved Dad, for loving
me unconditionally as a child and being my hero!

Family and friends, for supporting
me over the years with your presence,
encouragement, and spiritual guidance.

I thank God for choosing me for this project
while giving me His wisdom, knowledge,
and understanding to complete it.

CONTENTS

INTRODUCTION

Life can be full of many obstacles that we have to endure daily. Being divorced and raising two daughters alone was not a part of my future plan.

What happened? How did my
fairy-tale ending dissipate?

I told God, "This is not what You promised me in Your Word, and I deserve to be happy just like everyone else!" God spoke to me and said, "Your mind-set of having a fairy-tale marriage is fictitious and stems from a worldly mind-set." Happiness is a feeling, but joy is everlasting when it comes from a deep relationship with God!

I grew up believing that my handsome Prince Charming would sweep me off my feet and we would live happily ever after. I have been divorced for ten years now and have one daughter who is a sophomore in college and another daughter who is a sophomore in high school, but God sustained me through it all.

It's only by God's grace, unmerited favor, and goodness that I could overcome the many obstacles that I had to endure as a process of my journey to get me to the next level in my faith. God kept me and He allowed me to persevere through long-suffering, heartache, rejection, anger, bitterness, bad decisions, financial issues, job layoffs, and family issues. But I'm still here.

Life happened for me, and that brought about many negative emotions that led to anxiety and not feeling loved.

My beloved dad passed away when I was only twelve years old. His passing was devastating for me because we had developed a deep, fruitful father-daughter bond. I knew without a shadow of a doubt that my dad loved me. I can remember coming home from middle school and hoping he was already at home. He would take me to the meat market and other places with him. I enjoyed hanging out with him too. I began to miss him as the years went on, and I continued to ponder about what my life would reflect if he were still alive, especially when I was preparing for my first sermon.

The loss of my dad was the first time that I experienced grief and a broken heart. The void of my dad led me to make many bad decisions, especially when dating someone, but now I'm able to make godly decisions by asking God for His permission on how to proceed with any issue in my life.

It took many years for me to heal from my dad's death. Now I am able to embrace God's unconditional love for me and finally experience my true fulfillment as a single parent woman.

God will recycle everything that you have endured and allow you to have a powerful, life-changing testimony to bless others. God turned my pain from my dad's death and other hurtful experiences into a divine purpose so that He could receive the glory out of my life.

This book was written specifically to encourage single-parent women to press for the mark and not give up during the course of their journey. I pray that this book will spiritually encourage, guide, and give you the necessary tools for being successful as a single-parent after many series of hurts, disappointments, misfortunes, and especially a broken relationship. God has an awesome plan and purpose for your life. Today, you can start living on *purpose* by being healed of your past hurts and set free through Christ with *victory*!

CHAPTER 1

Starting Over: How to Move Forward

M oving forward requires you to ask yourself the tough questions and accept where God has placed you in this season.

Your marriage or relationship did not work, but God still has a plan for you! Don't give up or throw in the towel, because the enemy wants you to have a defeated spirit and make you lose hope in Christ! The enemy's goal is to make you as miserable and uncomfortable as possible, so don't allow him to have that much control over your life.

Everything happens for a reason in our lives. I was so disappointed in God too, but you don't have to go through this alone. God allows us to endure heartache to build our character and gain preparation to fulfill His will for our lives.

We will have many challenging circumstances, but it is our reaction that indicates growth. Only God can fight your battles! Until you work on this daily, you will always be an emotional mess. Some days you will get it right, and other days, you will fail the test. I have miserably failed many tests, but I have learned from my experiences that allowed me to grow in Christ. Your experiences will allow you to fulfill your purpose, which brings you peace and joy, in spite of what you're feeling.

> How should I react when my world seems to be crumbling down right before my eyes?

I reacted with anger and bitterness, which was unacceptable. I took my frustration out on people without being aware of it. I had to go through the full process of being healed from a marriage that abruptly ended.

These were a few of the many questions that I had occupying my mind during and after my divorce:

> Who can I lean on? Who can I trust during this season? Now that I am divorced, what will people say about me? How can I make it on my own now?

I had no clue how to begin my life as a single parent because that wasn't my plan. I felt defeated, disappointed, and like a failure.

I didn't tell anyone about my marital issues because I was praying and seeking understanding from God. I realized later that I should have sought biblical counseling because going at it alone was not healthy for me. You must have a spiritual person or counselor who will help you in this process, which helps you to be well-balanced, especially when you have negative emotions.

I felt as though the world was against me because of my failed marriage. I thought that I had made the correct decision with the mate who chose me, but I didn't ask God for permission to marry this person.

I didn't do my spiritual homework because I didn't understand God's design for marriage. I was clueless on what a spiritual marriage should reflect and how to be a helpmate. It may seem like failure, but it's only a small part of your very hopeful and prosperous journey.

Once I sought to gain a deeper relationship with God by consuming more of the Bible and meditating on key Scriptures that spoke to my spirit, God moved in my life by changing my thought patterns.

How did this relationship/marriage go wrong?

Don't allow past regrets to consume your life. There is life after a divorce and you can still live a life in *abundance.* God will restore everything that was taken from you, not material possessions, but *joy, peace, hope,* and most of all, *understanding!* You will dance in the rain again, but allow God to use this time to rebuild you spiritually.

Don't let the past catch up with your future. Move toward your prosperous, bright future. You're a diamond in the rough! A great work in progress! Don't listen to the enemies' lies because he has no authority over your life! You can have *victory* through Christ Jesus!

You must make peace with your situation. We have no control over what happens to us or the people who cross our paths with the wrong motives.

Having peace makes you an overall greater person to be around. No one wants to be in the presence of a negative person who talks about their breakup or divorce every time you see them. Focus on talking about positive topics unless you're seeing a biblical counselor.

God will allow the enemy to expose your actions for public viewing. Someone is waiting to see you get out of character and act foolish. We shouldn't necessarily care about what others think of us, but we don't want to tarnish our witness or testimony for Christ, either. We must watch how we are perceived by others.

"Therefore let us not pass judgment
on one another any longer, but rather
decide never to put a stumbling block or
hindrance in the way of a brother."
Romans 14:13

> How do you want to be perceived
> by your children?

Sometimes, I vented in front of my daughters because I was stressed out. When you are doing most of the running around, it can take a toll on you mentally and physically if you are not careful. Sometimes, I just wanted a mental break to get away from everything.

You should learn from your mistakes, ask God for guidance on how to pick up the broken pieces and heal you. Call out to Him daily, especially when you can't get out of the bed or have to meet with your ex for the sake of the children, and when you encounter his friends and family. God will give you a higher strength to carry on. Allow Him to take you under the shelter of His wings by showering you with His mercy and grace.

Whatever mistakes you have made thus far, you are forgiven, and God still loves you unconditionally with His agape love. Agape love means there's nothing in return and you don't have to work for it because this type of love is given *freely* by God. God will make you whole and complete again, so don't focus on the guilt, rejection, fear, and feeling shameful. God's love for you will never change.

You will go through these emotions, but take your journey one day at a time. God will allow you to observe change in how you handle your unresolved emotions.

Surround yourself with people who support you. They should have your best interest at heart, care about your well-being, desire to see you healed, and make sure you have the *victory* through Christ!

Nevertheless, we all have some people in our lives who are haters. I have always tried to see good in everyone, but some people have proved me wrong. I have allowed family members and others to mistreat me, but God showed me their motives and their jealous and deceitful spirits.

Be very careful who you share your personal struggles with. I shared with a family member at a very low point in my life, and they used it against me in anger. They tried to make me relive what I had experienced, but they didn't realize that I was healed from that wound.

I have concluded that when people are not happy, they don't want you to be happy either! *Misery loves company!* Set yourself free by treating others better than they treat you. Also, shower them in love because *love* conquers all! This does not mean that they will be in your space, but sometimes we must love people from a distance, or back away until we can handle them in a Christ-like manner.

Moving forward requires quiet time with God to seek His will for your life and clarity for your future. You should seek to put God first in your life. He should be on a higher level than anyone on this earth, and you should rely on Him for every aspect of your life!

> What should be my first step moving
> toward my total healing?

Personal Notes:

_____

_____

_____

_____

_____

_____

_____

_____

_____

_____

_____

_____

_____

_____

_____

_____

_____

_____

_____

_____

_____

_____

_____

_____

_____

_____

_____

_____

_____

_____

_____

_____

_____

_____

_____

_____

I can pick up all of the broken pieces by trusting
God wholeheartedly with my future!

CHAPTER 2

Healing from Your Past
Hurts and Wounds

Healing from your past hurts and wounds is required to begin a fruitful and blessed life. As a newly single parent, you should diligently work toward being totally free through Christ. You can harbor your feelings and emotions and not realize it until you have a major outburst of anger that will have a very negative effect on others. This means you have a heart issue that is rooted in your unresolved feelings from your past experiences. We can't truly love someone unless we are healed; otherwise, we are in denial by thinking that we are okay. We can't have joy for others when we are miserable.

To survive your walk as a believer, you must be selective of what you allow to enter your spirit. Make sure that you guard your heart from anything that has the potential to hurt you or prevent you from fulfilling your purpose.

"Above all else, guard your heart, for
everything you do flows from it."
Proverbs 4:23

Losing someone you loved can be devastating, especially if you did everything within your power to make the relationship work and it still failed. Don't think that you weren't good enough because God sees you as very special and a work in progress. Don't listen to the lies from the enemy. Satan will make us think negatively about ourselves, but God says that you are perfect in the way that He has created you.

"I praise you because I am fearfully
and wonderfully made; your works are
wonderful, I know that full well."
Psalm 139:14

"Be perfect, therefore, as your
heavenly Father is perfect."
Matthew 5:48

First, you must work toward being healed from the letdowns, disappointments, unmet expectations, and your high expectations of others. I used to expect people to act a certain way, which only made life more difficult for me. You can overcome this by completely depending and trusting God with the decisions that you make. You must control your negative emotions because they do have a powerful influence on your entire life and they affect your approach and reaction to people.

Negative Emotions List:
Anger
Jealously
Controlling
Anxious
Demanding
Hopelessness
Guilt
Frustrated
Untrusting
Secretive
Passive
Shutting down
Unforgiving
Negative
Confused
Irresponsible

Our emotions can give us highs of feeling wonderful, ready to conquer the world like Wonder Woman, and lows of feeling sad and hopeless where the world seems to be coming to an end for us.

You ultimately have complete control of what you say and your actions. Don't make excuses for bad behavior, because as you grow in Christ, there should be something different about you that sets you apart from the world. I used to allow people to push my buttons, but today, it's much easier because God gives me discernment to recognize what's about to transpire. When I feel a negative vibe from someone, I know that I need to be still or take a few seconds before I respond. We don't have to be a part of the worldly standards because we are God's ambassadors and we represent *Him*. We are the first person someone may see in certain settings, and we must be obedient to the Holy Spirit.

> *"For the Lord will carry out his sentence*
> *on earth with speed and finality."*
> Romans 9:28

Unfortunately, we are the product of our upbringing, and everything about us as adults reflects our childhood experiences. We can't choose our parents or relatives, but at the end of the day, we don't have to mimic their behavior by taking our issues out on others.

When you know better, you should do better, meaning that you should strive to be your best daily for your overall well-being and for your children. If you are not careful, your childhood experiences can show up in your adult relationships, especially a marriage. Some of our negative experiences as children were due to improper parenting; therefore, we should stop mimicking these negative behaviors.

Unresolved issues from your childhood can be detrimental to all of your relationships. You must find a place of peace so that you can take control of your feelings and emotions. You must work at this daily and for the rest of your journey. Growth and maturity occurs when we think about our actions and correct them immediately. If we are doing the same thing every day with the same negative results, now is the time for change.

Don't allow people to be in control of how you feel because of their unkind words or actions. God is *powerful*, He is the *higher* source, and He should be the authoritative figure over your life.

When you invite God into your heart daily, you become equipped to handle people and situations spiritually. That little voice that you hear is the Holy Spirit trying to warn you of something or give you instruction.

"And the peace of God, which transcends
all understanding, will guard your hearts
and your minds in Christ Jesus."
Philippians 4:7

God will give you the ultimate peace while allowing you to be content in every situation. Feelings are normal as long as you don't stay stuck in your feelings. You must recognize when the negative feelings arise and seek God for guidance.

> Why am I feeling this way? Where is this coming from? What is the root of this feeling?

Prayer:

> God, help me to deal with my feelings
> spiritually right now!

Don't allow people to take the frustrations of their past hurts on you. This is not walking in love or showing love to you. So many people in the world are not healed. Don't be a doormat for an unhealed person. Pray for their healing by asking God to expose the root of the issues in their life with conviction.

Letting go of the past is also key to your healing process. Give everything to God to handle, and don't allow yourself to block your blessings. You can be your worst enemy, and God does not need your assistance.

> *"Then they cried to the Lord in their trouble,*
> *and he saved them from their distress.*
> *He sent out his word and healed them;*

he rescued them from the grave."
Psalm 107: 19–20

"Peace I leave with you; my peace I give you. I
do not give to you as the world gives. Do not let
your hearts be troubled and do not be afraid."
John 14:27

God will restore you and make your heart whole again. Allow yourself to go through this process, because in time, God will reveal why He allowed these circumstances to manifest in your life.

God is always at work behind the scenes, working everything out for your good. Your story has not ended just yet! God still desires the *best* for you!

You must take the time to grieve the loss of someone who was very dear to you. You may have spent many countless hours with this person, including phone calls, text messages, and one-on-one time. Losing someone from a breakup or divorce requires you to grieve.

Don't ignore the signs of your grief, which are denial, anger, bargaining, depression, and finally, acceptance. You will go through these stages repeatedly. Sometimes skipping one emotion and going to the next, but you can experience all of them daily.

Depression occurs after days of being in a deep, dark place with your negative, misleading thoughts. Trust God, even for your grieving process, and yield every concern to Him. You don't have to have sleepless nights when God is up 24/7 rooting for you.

God wants to use you as a tool to bless others, but you must have a whole heart before He can trust you. Start living on purpose for His glory and walk into your destiny! Don't allow the enemy to derail God's plan because you have allowed your pain to manifest so deeply that God can't use you. We are all called to serve God in some type of capacity for His kingdom.

> What are you called to do? Why are you
> running from your calling? Are you tired
> of running? Why are you afraid?

Personal Notes:

_____

_____

_____

_____

_____

_____

_____

_____

_____

_____

_____

_____

_____

_____

_____

_____

_____

_____

_____

I am healed by God with a whole heart!

CHAPTER 3

The Power
of Forgiveness

An unforgiving spirit is a very dangerous lifestyle! We should not hold others hostage in our minds by reacting with negative actions because of their wrongdoings toward us. They may have said something hurtful or broke up with you, but allowing someone to be free from your judgmental spirit will set you free too.

Most of the time, we hold on to the wrongdoing because it was a horrible experience or devastating to us, but this will only allow us to be miserable. We can't focus on God by giving people so much negative attention. We must shift our focus off of those people and allow God to rightfully handle them. God knows exactly how to handle them, not you. If you focus on the spirit of forgiveness, you will have an inner peace.

Forgiveness is very powerful! It releases all of the unwanted negative emotions. God has forgiven you several times, and you should forgive others too.

> *"Then Peter came to Jesus and asked, "Lord,*
> *how many times shall I forgive my brother*
> *or sister who sins against me? Up to seven*
> *times. Jesus answered, "I tell you, not*
> *seven times, but seventy-seven times."*
> *Matthew 18:21–22*

We are commanded by God to forgive others!

It took me years to finally be at peace once people wronged me, especially family and friends. But once I focused on God instead of them, there was instant change in my thinking.

Don't hold grudges against people. They have most likely moved on with their lives, and you are still allowing them to take up space in your mind. This type of thinking keeps you from being in God's presence daily, and it can block your blessings.

When you have an unforgiving spirit, this causes undue stress and eventually health issues for you.

Focus on God and not the person!

> Is the issue or person worth your time
> and energy? Could you utilize this time
> for God or your children instead?

No one should steal your joy if you are praying daily for a forgiving spirit. Forgiveness is healing for your body, soul, and spirit. God desires for you to be complete without a broken heart or spirit. When we don't forgive others, we become defeated in our spirits.

When you forgive, you trust God, and no matter how you feel about the person or situation, you give the issue over to Him.

Forgiveness is a learned spiritual behavior only by experience. It prompts you to stop holding on to the offense and allows you to take the person out of jail and stop pronouncing them guilty as charged. There is power in the healing process if you remove yourself from the equation and allow God to move on His timing.

"For if you forgive other people when they sin against you, your heavenly Father will also forgive you. But if you do not forgive others their sins, your Father will not forgive your sins."
Matthew 6:14–15

Refusing to forgive is a sin against God. We should trust God for justice and forgive the person who offended us. This does not mean we must forget the offense, either, but we let the person off the hook.

"It is mine to avenge; I will repay. In due time their foot will slip; their day of disaster is near and their doom rushes upon them."
Deuteronomy 32:35

"We are witnesses of everything he did in the country of the Jews and in Jerusalem. They killed him by hanging him on a cross, but God raised him from the dead on the third day and caused him to be seen. He was not seen by all the people, but by witnesses whom God had already chosen—by us who ate and drank with him after He rose from the dead. He commanded us to preach to the people and to testify that he is the one whom God appointed as judge of the living and the dead. All the prophets testify about him that everyone who believes in him receives forgiveness of sins through his name."
Acts 10:39–43

We are all wounded and inadequate at some point in our lives. On our best days, our self-esteem juggles between feeble and fragile. It only takes a disapproval or perceived disapproval to send us wavering and fretting in our ways. These attacks bother us because we forget who we are in Christ. Don't allow the enemy to trick you with his schemes.

We are lovingly adopted into God's royal family as His daughters once we are saved by becoming a believer. Our true worth comes from our relationship with God, not from our appearance, performance, net worth, or affiliates.

We seek others' approval, and when they reject us, it hurts badly. When we take our eyes off of God and His acceptance and place them on the conditional acceptance of our boss, spouse, or friends, we set ourselves up to be hurt. We forget that some people are incapable of showing others love because of their past experiences. Only by experience do we become closer to God and learn how to love more.

We are to forgive so that we may appreciate God's goodness without feeling the burden of anger sweltering within our hearts. Forgiveness does not mean we recant the fact that what happened to us was wrong. Instead, we roll our burdens onto the Lord and allow Him to carry them for us.

Do you have an unforgiving spirit? Why?

We have heart issues and mask so much about our true selves, especially our many flaws and mistakes. We want to be perceived by the world as being perfect, but God is saying "take your mask off" because He already knows every detail about you. I will expound on this later in the book. Again, with *prayer*, God can heal you through the forgiveness.

Joseph humbled himself and remained faithful to God for thirteen years even though his brothers sold him into slavery because of their jealous ways. He was accused of rape by Potiphar's wife because he wouldn't accept her sexual advances, which landed him in jail. God blessed Joseph for his prayers, patience, endurance, and unshakable faith. He became second in command in Egypt, and still blessed his brothers that sinned against him. Joseph did not throw in the towel, instead he trusted God wholeheartedly.

I can relate to Joseph because of my past hurts and pain from people while going through life issues. I wanted to give up many times, but my faith in God would not allow me to throw in the towel. I've learned to take my journey one moment at a time and to trust God, no matter how bad my circumstances may appear. Joseph is a perfect example of love and forgiveness!

*"Jacob lived in the land where his father
had stayed, the land of Canaan. This is
the account of Jacob's family line.*

*Joseph, a young man of seventeen, was tending
the flocks with his brothers, the sons of Bilhah
and the sons of Zilpah, his father's wives, and he
brought their father a bad report about them.*

*Now Israel loved Joseph more than any of his
other sons, because he had been born to him
in his old age; and he made an ornate robe for
him. When his brothers saw that their father
loved him more than any of them, they hated
him and could not speak a kind word to him.*

*Joseph had a dream, and when he told it to his
brothers, they hated him all the more. He said to
them, 'Listen to this dream I had: We were binding
sheaves of grain out in the field when suddenly my
sheaf rose and stood upright, while your sheaves
gathered around mine and bowed down to it.'*

*His brothers said to him, 'Do you intend to
reign over us? Will you actually rule us?'
And they hated him all the more because
of his dream and what he had said.*

*Then he had another dream, and he told it to
his brothers. 'Listen,' he said, I had another
dream, and this time the sun and moon and
eleven stars were bowing down to me.'*

*When he told his father as well as his brothers,
his father rebuked him and said, 'What is this
dream you had? Will your mother and I and
your brothers actually come and bow down to the
ground before you?' His brothers were jealous of
him, but his father kept the matter in mind.*

*Now his brothers had gone to graze their father's
flocks near Shechem, and Israel said to Joseph, 'As
you know, your brothers are grazing the flocks near
Shechem. Come, I am going to send you to them.'*

'Very well,' he replied.

*So he said to him, 'Go and see if all is well with your
brothers and with the flocks, and bring word back to
me.' Then he sent him off from the Valley of Hebron.*

*When Joseph arrived at Shechem, a man
found him wandering around in the fields
and asked him, 'What are you looking for?'*

*He replied, 'I'm looking for my brothers. Can you
tell me where they are grazing their flocks?'*

*'They have moved on from here,' the man answered.
'I heard them say, "Let's go to Dothan."'*

*So Joseph went after his brothers and found them
near Dothan. But they saw him in the distance, and
before he reached them, they plotted to kill him.*

*'Here comes that dreamer!' they said to each
other. 'Come now, let's kill him and throw
him into one of these cisterns and say that
a ferocious animal devoured him. Then
we'll see what comes of his dreams.'*

*When Reuben heard this, he tried to rescue
him from their hands. 'Let's not take his life,'
he said. 'Don't shed any blood. Throw him into
this cistern here in the wilderness, but don't lay
a hand on him.' Reuben said this to rescue him
from them and take him back to his father.*

*So when Joseph came to his brothers, they stripped
him of his robe—the ornate robe he was wearing—
and they took him and threw him into the cistern.
The cistern was empty; there was no water in it.*

*As they sat down to eat their meal, they looked
up and saw a caravan of Ishmaelites coming
from Gilead. Their camels were loaded with
spices, balm and myrrh, and they were on
their way to take them down to Egypt.*

*Judah said to his brothers, 'What will we gain
if we kill our brother and cover up his blood?
Come, let's sell him to the Ishmaelites and not
lay our hands on him; after all, he is our brother,
our own flesh and blood.' His brothers agreed.*

*So when the Midianite merchants came by,
his brothers pulled Joseph up out of the cistern
and sold him for twenty shekels of silver to
the Ishmaelites, who took him to Egypt.*

*When Reuben returned to the cistern and saw
that Joseph was not there, he tore his clothes.
He went back to his brothers and said, 'The
boy isn't there! Where can I turn now?'*

*Then they got Joseph's robe, slaughtered a goat and
dipped the robe in the blood. They took the ornate
robe back to their father and said, 'We found this.
Examine it to see whether it is your son's robe.'*

He recognized it and said, 'It is my son's robe! Some ferocious animal has devoured him. Joseph has surely been torn to pieces.'

Then Jacob tore his clothes, put on sackcloth and mourned for his son many days. All his sons and daughters came to comfort him, but he refused to be comforted. 'No,' he said, 'I will continue to mourn until I join my son in the grave.' So his father wept for him.

Meanwhile, the Midianites sold Joseph in Egypt to Potiphar, one of Pharaoh's officials, the captain of the guard."
Genesis 37:1–36

> Can you forgive a family member and forget about the offense? Why?

> Are you willing to ask a family member to forgive you?

Truly being set free is letting go of all your past hurts and wounds while growing from them so that you can live an abundant life. If you are holding on to past issues from years ago, I pray that God will heal you and set you free while giving you a whole heart.

Give the person back to Christ daily because He can only change their hearts for the better, and it's not our responsibility. So, go to sleep at night and rest in Him.

Prayer:

Father God, I give _____ back to you today! I'm healed of anything that was done to me as a child, teenager, or adult. _____ is your son/ daughter, and they are rightfully yours, not mine. You are in control, not me.

God, take care of their heart and heal my heart in the process. I take _____ out of the cage because you, Father, You can handle them, change their ways, and convict them to repent of their sins.

Let me not continue to play it over in my mind, but I release this to you today for once and for all. I thank you for the victory and the testimony to bless others.

In Jesus's name, I pray. Amen.

> What did you learn from this chapter
> that is beneficial for your future?

Personal Notes:

_____

_____

_____

_____

_____

_____

_____

_____

_____

_____

_____

_____

_____

_____

_____

_____

_____

_____

_____

_____

_____

_____

_____

_____

DESOLYN L. HICKS

_____
_____
_____
_____
_____
_____
_____
_____
_____
_____
_____
_____
_____
_____
_____
_____
_____
_____
_____
_____
_____
_____
_____
_____

I forgive those who have hurt me,
and I release them to God!

CHAPTER 4

Parent Wisdom

As single parents, we should use our valuable time to nurture our children to be godly and follow their purpose while impacting society as adults.

"Children are a heritage from the LORD,
offspring a reward from him."
Psalm 127:3

"Your wife will be like a fruitful vine
within your house; your children will be
like olive shoots around your table."
Psalm 128:3

A parent's responsibility is to sow positive seeds into their children with words of encouragement, affirmation, by sharing God's promises, and, teaching them about hope in Jesus Christ, which will lead them to have an intimate relationship with Him as a believer. Our children should feel loved by us and know that we will support them in every situation, bad or good. I have messed up many times in this area, so I allowed room for failure and asked God for a greater understanding daily while parenting.

Your first ministry is at home before you serve God in other areas of your life. You should have Bible lessons and prayer with your children. You should pray over them as they sleep at night. Sunday worship and fellowship are required by God, but our children should learn God's Word from us first. Don't rely on the church to be the only avenue for them to learn about Jesus.

Prayer:

Prayer is a key component of our walk with Christ, and we should make it a priority. We must keep our children covered by asking God to dispatch His angels to watch over them, allow them to make godly, wise decisions by selecting godly friends, and obey and respect us as the authoritative figure in their lives. We should not parent as an army drill sergeant, but with forgiveness, unconditional love, and providing them grace.

Accountability:

We are held accountable as parents if we continue to make the same mistakes. When you mess up, God should convict you so profoundly that you will instantly recognize your shortcomings as a parent. No one is a perfect parent, even if a person claims to be. Most women want to be perceived by others as being perfect because it makes them appear to be Superwoman, when in reality, we all have the same struggles.

Extracurricular Activities:

In my opinion, our children should not have more than two extracurricular activities because we will be overwhelmed with the hustle and bustle of balancing our families with work, church, school, projects, and other activities. Society says that our children are better students when they are involved in many activities, but I disagree. We should use our own judgment by praying about it first before we make any decisions concerning them. We can't go by worldly standards and must choose God's standards.

Our children should be challenged in a positive way. Maybe allow them to join one church ministry and one activity at school, but overloading them with activities can be exhausting for you as well.

I have noticed that some parents welcome many activities because it makes them feel important and they want to receive the accolades. This is distorted thinking and a deep-rooted issue that has to be prayed about.

Some parents want to live out their dreams through their children, and this is not fair to them. We had our time, and now it's time for our children to blossom. Stop putting your dreams on your children because they can't live up to your expectations. Continued unmet expectations can lead to an array of heartfelt issues that you don't want them to endure in life.

> Is anything from your past allowing you to overcompensate through your children?

Discipline:

Discipline starts at home, not in the grocery store or the mall. Our children should be well-rounded individuals, but with boundaries, not doing as they please, and not disrespecting us as parents, either. I have witnessed so many parents being disrespected in public and I am embarrassed for the parents. Most of all, we should not use abuse but wise discipline.

*"Start children off on the way they should go, and
even when they are old they will not turn from it."*
Proverbs 22:6

Also, everyone is not a straight A student. God will give us a glimpse of our children's gifts, and we should pray about these gifts and allow them to manifest by coaching them with the right approach. Discern your children's potential and build on their gifts daily, not molding them to be what you think they should be but what God desires for them to become.

My younger daughter has a gift of applying makeup, and I have encouraged her to take a class, obtain a part-time job, or do makeup once she attends college and charge a small fee. My older daughter has gifts of public speaking and acting that were revealed when she was in high school. Recently, I asked her what she was doing with crafting her gift. She said she had pushed these gifts aside due to college and focusing on her career once she graduates. I asked her to pray about them and God will open doors for her to utilize her gifts.

We should encourage our children to bring their gifts forth for God's glory and not bully them into doing things our way so that we will gain self-gratification.

God has all the answers when it comes to being a parent. Everything that we need or an answer to any concern can be found in the Bible. Again, it is crucial to seek God always for any decisions that we make for our children. Don't be hard on yourself when you make mistakes, because you are learning as you continue to parent and becoming stronger, better, and wiser in the process.

> *"And without faith it is impossible to please*
> *God, because anyone who comes to him*
> *must believe that he exists and that he*
> *rewards those who earnestly seek him."*
> *Hebrews 11:6*

All children were created differently by God, and this is what sets us apart as individuals and allows us to be unique in our own way! They may have similarities, but we should never compare them to each other or to us, which can be a detrimental experience and cause major emotional issues later.

> *"Above all else, guard your heart, for*
> *everything you do flows from it."*
> *Proverbs 4:23*

Comparing your children to other people can create a lifelong feeling of not being good enough and cause them to go through life trying to please everyone, thinking that they have to be accepted by society and live up to your expectations. This type of thinking will spill over into other relationships, which is not healthy.

I grew up with a parent who showed certain siblings favoritism, and this created a wedge in our relationship. It took years for me to overcome this stronghold. We don't realize the massive effect that this type of behavior can have on our children when they become adults.

When we make mistakes, we should recognize our faults and apologize to our children. When we cross the line and allow the wrong attitude to take root, resentment starts to creep into their hearts. Growing up in my era, parents did not admit wrongdoings, but as a parent, I quickly recognized that some of my actions were not acts of love. I should be the prime example for my children and operate in love daily. It's the same agape love that God shows us daily, and no matter how bad we mess up, He shows us His undeserving grace as well.

> *"I prayed for this child, and the LORD has granted me what I asked of him. So now I give him to the LORD. For his whole life he will be given over to the Lord.' And he worshiped the LORD there."*
> *1 Samuel 1:27–28*

Lastly, discipline is an important factor in nurturing our children, which can be a challenge at some points, but the key is to be consistent. Once you make a decision, don't deviate from your plan of action.

Again, every child is different, so what works for one child will not necessarily work for the other.

Our children must learn that there are consequences for their actions, and when they become adults, the stakes are even greater. If you expect them to become productive adults with boundaries and be able to maintain a full-time job without being a disruptive employee, then it's time to go to work and invest in your children's future. We must exercise discipline. God's Word teaches us to.

> *"Whoever spares the rod hates their children, but the one who loves their children is careful to discipline them."*
> *Proverbs 13:24*

These Scriptures reveal that we must teach our children how to act at home and in public. Whether it's at church, school, or the White House, they should know how to conduct themselves. If you have disrespectful children who won't follow the rules, you are responsible, not anyone else. *Stop* blaming other people for your undisciplined children. You're not their best friend, but their loving parent! If you truly love your child, you will make sure you raise them with godly principles, and not making up your own principles along the way.

We should be praying for our children's total well-being, including the future.

Daily prayer for our children:

God bless _____'s future. Allow him/her to be a spiritual, productive, and prosperous member of society through You while serving You with gladness. He/she will be a blessing to many. Keep him/her surrounded with godly friends. Give him/her a higher level of discernment. Let him/her not be deceived by the trick of the enemy. _____ has a calling on his/her life. Allow it to manifest on Your time, for Your glory, and Your kingdom.

The enemy knows what God has planned for our children, and his job is to derail it. Be very proactive in securing their future by praying His promises for their lives.

> How can you obtain God's wisdom daily for every decision that you make? What's your first step?

DESOLYN L. HICKS

Personal Notes:

_____

_____

_____

_____

_____

_____

_____

_____

_____

_____

_____

_____

_____

_____

_____

_____

_____

_____

_____

_____

_____

_____

_____

_____

_____
_____
_____
_____
_____
_____
_____
_____
_____
_____
_____
_____
_____
_____
_____
_____
_____
_____
_____
_____
_____
_____
_____

God's Word will be my guideline
for raising my children!

CHAPTER 5

Sacrifice Over
Selfish Desires

W e should never put anyone before our children but God because this could have a negative impact on their lives in the future.

Sacrifice means relinquishing something dear to us to acquire something greater, such as important relationships. We should shower our children with unconditional love by putting their needs before ours. It's the same love that Christ extends to us daily.

I wanted to be a pharmaceutical sales representative, but God showed me that traveling and being away from my girls was not His plan and that I needed to put this desire on hold. This desire has been on hold indefinitely because a few years later, I was called to serve in a higher capacity in ministry. God always has a greater plan for us! Be careful of holding on to your dreams and plans, because God can strip them away at any time. I'm elated that I did not pursue this career, because my girls would not have received the appropriate attention and bonding that was necessary for their growth.

My daughters mean the world to me, and I feel blessed that God has trusted me to care for them in a very special way. Motherhood is a gift from God. Don't take it for granted; ask God for a practical, spiritual approach to each child.

Be careful of what type of job you are willing to accept. Sometimes a lower paying job is more suitable for your kids' schedule and you must *sacrifice* for their sake. The world says that we have to be in a high-income bracket, drive a certain type of car, live in a large home, and save money for the future because it's the American dream. A lie from the pit of hell! These are all false misconceptions. God's perspective is not gaining materialistic things for self-gratification, competing with others, or having bragging rights of what you own. Pray about where God desires for you to be employed. God can provide and take your salary and work miracles with it, but you must ask Him to help you to be a good steward of your money also.

Being in a relationship proved to be very difficult for me while nurturing my girls. Single parents really don't have a personal life because our children take up most of our time. When we sacrifice for our children, we will reap the benefits later in life.

I could have done some things differently. The gentleman that I dated wanted a lot of my time, but I just didn't have the free time that he expected of me. Dishonesty crept into the relationship, and eventually, I had to walk away, which was painful.

Sacrificing was not always easy for me, but if I didn't put my daughters first, my lack of parenting would have resurfaced later in their actions and decisions. You will never have perfect children because you are not a perfect mother, but sacrifice is key to a fruitful, blessed home.

> *"Every good and perfect gift is from above, coming down from the Father of the heavenly lights, who does not change like shifting shadows."*
> *James 1:17*

We can't focus on ourselves and expect great results in the end. A prime example of this is not studying for a test and expecting to receive an excellent score for showing up. Do the work that's necessary to raise your children with the fear and reverence of God.

Our children need us! We can't go back and redo anything once they are grown. Just focus on the present by sacrificing for them, and God will take care of their future.

"For the flesh desires what is contrary to the Spirit, and the Spirit what is contrary to the flesh. They are in conflict with each other, so that you are not to do whatever you want."
Galatians 5:17

Do not allow the enemy to attack your mind with the mistakes that you made. God has given us the power to conquer our flesh and feed our spiritual side with His Word, prayer, et cetera. He will always give us a way of escape if we listen to His voice.

The enemy will use your selfish desires to neglect your family. God has blessed you with beautiful children, but sometimes we get distracted and prefer to hang out rather than nurture them as a parent. Honestly, there's nothing wrong with going out sometimes, but every weekend can be extreme and this is not showing love. If being away supersedes your quality time with your children, this is not sacrifice. Again, I am not a perfect parent, but I grew from my experiences and learned how to sacrifice for my children by relying on God's wisdom.

Please choose sacrifice over your own desires because once you become an empty nester, God will give you a new season of celebration.

What is your main priority?

How can you focus on God with distractions?

Personal Notes:

_____

_____

_____

_____

_____

_____

_____

_____

_____

_____

_____

_____

_____

_____

_____

_____

_____

_____

_____

_____

_____
_____
_____
_____
_____
_____
_____
_____
_____
_____
_____
_____
_____
_____
_____
_____
_____
_____
_____
_____
_____
_____
_____

I will sacrifice for my children and
yield my selfish desires to Christ!

CHAPTER 6

Focus on God

Focusing on God means to meditate on His Word, attend Bible study, and pray daily to set the spiritual foundation for your life! Also, fasting should be incorporated, especially when you need a desperate change in your life. This will allow you not to be anxious and seek God for a profound answer. These tools will allow you to build an intimate relationship with God, which ultimately gives you peace, joy, and unshakable faith.

As believers, our faith should be our solid foundation because without faith, we are hopeless, but with God, *all* things are possible.

> *"Jesus looked at them and said, 'With man this is impossible, but with God all things are possible.'"*
> *Matthew 19:26*

The Bible is our blueprint for life, and we should have Scriptures embedded in our hearts for times of trouble. When you have Scriptures in your spirit, you can conquer anything that's out of your control. Our faith foundation is the root of our existence.

God desires a one-on-one relationship with you. He has your best interest at heart, and most of all, He is concerned about your well-being. Having a deep, fulfilled spiritual connection with God allows you to be able to deal with the issues in your life.

The enemy is very crafty and his main position is to kill, steal, and destroy families in any way possible.

"The thief comes only to steal and kill and destroy; I have come that they may have life, and have it to the full."
John 10:10

Our spirits must be nourished daily with the Word of God so that we will remain in His presence, which will allow us to have positive thoughts daily.

I listen to Dr. Charles Stanley every day while preparing for work. Sometimes I stop to take notes if he says something powerful to my spirit. This is my devotion before I hit the road for work, which sets the tone for my day. My spirit is then free of clutter and negative thoughts that I may have woken up with.

When I was enrolled at the College of Biblical Studies, the devil would convince me that I needed a job and money. He had a grip on me, and I would fret, grow weary, and well up with anxiety. I would take my morning run after my daughter went to school and when I sat down in my study to work on my assignments, negative thoughts would consume my mind. After being in the devil's trap a few times, I finally mastered how to overcome these awful thoughts. I had to leave my place and go to Starbucks or the library to escape the negative lies of the enemy. Make time to renew your mind daily, even if you have to set an alarm as a reminder to spend time with God.

The following Scriptures have kept me focused on God for many years, especially when I was going through difficult times.

For Strength:

> "The LORD is my shepherd, I lack
> nothing. He makes me lie down in green
> pastures, he leads me beside quiet waters,
> He refreshes my soul. He guides me along
> the right paths for his name's sake. Even
> though I walk through the darkest valley,
> I will fear no evil, for you are with me;
> your rod and your staff, they comfort me.

You prepare a table before me in the presence of my enemies. You anoint my head with oil; my cup overflows. Surely your goodness and love will follow me all the days of my life, and I will dwell in the house of the LORD forever."

Psalm 23

For Confidence in God:

"The LORD is my light and my salvation—whom shall I fear? The LORD is the stronghold of my life—of whom shall I be afraid?

When evil men advance against me to devour me, it is my enemies and my foes who will stumble and fall. Though an army besiege me, my heart will not fear; though war break out against me, even then will I be confident."

Psalm 27:1–3

For Enemies:

"Do not fret because of those who are evil or be envious of those who do wrong; for like the grass they will soon wither, like green plants they will soon die away.

Trust in the LORD and do good; dwell in the land and enjoy safe pasture. Take delight in the LORD, and he will give you the desires of your heart.

Commit your way to the LORD; trust in him and he will do this: He will make your righteous reward shine like the dawn your vindication like the noonday sun.

Be still before the LORD and wait patiently for him; do not fret when men succeed in their ways, when they carry out their wicked schemes.

Refrain from anger and turn from wrath; do not fret—it leads only to evil."

Psalm 37:1–8

Relying on God to speak to me was a life-changing experience, and you can have the same success also. He desires the best for you because you're the apple of His eye and you are a member of His royal priesthood. Our Father is the King and He knows every fine detail about you. So, walk with your head held high like the *queen* that God has called you to be.

When I need to focus on God and not my circumstances, I have a few inspirational sayings that I speak out loud:

> I'm focused, not swerved.
>
> I have a deliberate purpose.
>
> I have ambition.
>
> I have inner strength.
>
> I'm not needy.
>
> I'm not clingy.
>
> I yield my loneliness to God.
>
> I'm not insecure because I'm secure in Christ.
>
> God, I am the woman that You have called me to be!
>
> Allow me to walk wisely and step into Your will today!

Once I finish proclaiming these phrases, my mind is renewed and I feel God's presence immediately. Also, write down positive phrases, passages, or Scriptures and post them on your mirror, in your car, on the refrigerator, or even on your desk at work because this will keep you on track and your mind renewed when confusion arises. You must always be ready!

We must focus on God and not on our circumstances, because doubt begins to creep into our thoughts. The enemy will play the record repeatedly in our minds until it becomes the remix version. The enemy can plant one thought in your mind and then it becomes several thoughts, which takes your focus off of God.

I endured anxiety several years ago after my divorce because I had a fear that I was not going to succeed. I had to take medication to help me get through this tough period in my life, but with prayer and exercise, I overcame this demonic spirit by releasing my fears to God. Don't wait until things in your life begin to spiral out of control before you seriously seek God and trust His promises. God has given us an abundance of promises in the Bible, and they are still valid today because God's Word will never change!

Build your faith foundation now so that when trouble comes your way, you will know how to respond correctly instead of experiencing the roller coaster of never-ending emotions. As women, we can be up one minute and down the next because God made us special with emotions, but we must learn to control them. I failed miserably many times with my uncontrolled emotions, but I thank God for His extended grace in my life!

My sister, the Word of God will guide your steps by giving you sound instruction and allow you to make the right decisions with spiritual wisdom. His instruction can keep us from harm and warn us before making bad choices that have consequences later.

> *"Your word is a lamp for my*
> *feet, a light on my path."*
> Psalm 119:105

Does your character line up with your
walk with Christ? Why or why not?

> *"For this very reason, make every effort to*
> *add to your faith goodness; and to goodness,*
> *knowledge; and to knowledge, self-control;*
> *and to self-control, perseverance; and to*
> *perseverance, godliness; and to godliness, mutual*
> *affection, and to mutual affection, love."*
> 2 Peter 1:5–7

*"Therefore I tell you, whatever you ask
for in prayer, believe that you have
received it, and it will be yours."*
Mark 11:24

What steps can you take to
stay focused on God?

Personal Notes:

_____

_____

_____

_____

_____

_____

_____

_____

_____

_____

_____

_____

_____

_____

_____

_____

_____

_____

_____

_____

_____

_____

_____

_____

_____

_____

_____

_____

_____

_____

_____

_____

_____

_____

_____

_____

_____

_____

_____

_____

*I will focus on God and not allow
the enemy to distract me!*

CHAPTER 7

Finances

Finances can be an unpleasant topic to speak about, but we should yield our finances to God to grow with wisdom on how to manage our money.

Representatives from major credit card companies gave credit cards to freshmen in college, and all they had to do was sign their name on the dotted line. I received credit card offers in the mail while in college, and as you probably guessed, I applied for all of them. I had an American Express at nineteen years old and also acquired other credit cards, and I could barely pay the minimum amounts due monthly.

I was in debt at nineteen years old and working two part-time jobs while attending college. I had a lack of knowledge on how to handle my finances as a college student. My finances spiraled out of control.

It's not easy to rebuild credit once it has been ruined, but it is attainable. Don't apply for credit cards that you know you can't afford. Swiping a credit card feels marvelous at the height of purchasing of a new item, but fast forward, we eventually feel guilt and remorse because it wasn't the correct choice. When the credit card statements start arriving, you will most likely make the minimum payment, and this will leave you owing money for several years. I would suggest that you have one major credit card for emergency purposes only.

Today, most companies will check your credit as part of the background process for a job, and this could be the deal breaker for their decision to hire you. Companies want to make sure that you pay your bills on time and you are not a risk for them, especially if you will handle money.

If the decision was based on my credit report, I wouldn't have gotten one particular job after my divorce. I had to file for bankruptcy, and that was a difficult time for me.

Don't feel embarrassed if you have financial issues, because rich people have the same problems as well. Your testimony will be on how you were able to bounce back from your financial woes and learn from the experience. God is still at work even when we make financial mistakes because He desires the *best* for us, and as parents, we are responsible for teaching our children about finances.

"The rich rule over poor, and the
borrower is slave to the lender."
Proverbs 22:7

"Pride goes before destruction, a
haughty spirit before a fall."
Proverbs 16:18

Our upbringing has taught some of us that we should walk around with an S on our chest, pretending to be Superwoman, but there is a different story deeply rooted inside of us. We hide our financial woes to not be seen as weak before others.

Why do you hide your financial woes?
Could this be a pride issue for you?

The world says that if we aren't making a certain amount of money, then we're not blessed. This is not God's method. He declares for us to be content in *all* things, even with your current salary. God can work miracles with your salary if you ask for His advice on how to handle your funds monthly and prepare a budget. When you trust God totally with your finances, He will always prevail.

Also, remember that we should be tithing, but if you aren't, allow your heart to guide you on what you can give.

"'Bring the whole tithe into the storehouse, that there may be food in my house. Test me in this,' says the LORD *Almighty, 'and see if I will not throw open the floodgates of heaven and pour out so much blessing that there will not be room enough to store it.'"*
Malachi 3:10

Giving is not only focused on the church body, but also outside of the church walls. Our money is loaned to us by God to be a blessing to others. Giving could be in the form of buying someone coffee, a journal, lunch, et cetera. Also, you can give to a charity and donate food for needy people. These are all excellent forms of giving. Ask God how you should give to bless someone else.

"A generous person will prosper; whoever refreshes others will be refreshed."
Proverbs 11:25

We are commanded by God to be a blessing to others, and pouring into someone else should be a priority for us.

Hurricane Ike hit the Houston area in 2008. Our place took in an abundance of water, and we had to be relocated. A new friend and church member sent me money in the mail and she insisted that I purchase something for me. This was such a blessing because we went through so much with the move. She was an angel during my difficult time. She made an impact on my life with her kind gesture, and it has always remained in my spirit. We never know who God may use to bless us. Always be grateful and pay it forward by blessing someone else.

While in college earning my second degree, God made a way for my daughters and me because He wanted me to focus on my degree. I was not able to go outside of the realm of my bills and splurge at times, but I promised God that when He blessed me with a job, I would give more to others, and today I am doing this.

God will always put you in an unfamiliar space for Him to gain something major out of you, such as building your character and ultimately trusting Him more.

As the youngest girl of my family, I was spoiled, and my siblings would agree with me. I was very selfish because I was accustomed to having my way with my family.

Once I became an adult, these same traits started to resurface until a few people asked me, "Were you spoiled growing up?" That hurt my feelings, and I had to face reality. God immediately revealed to me that I had the wrong attitude and I was acting immature, which allowed me to take a closer look at myself. Feelings are always fleeting because they come and go. They don't last for a long period of time, and we can't stay stuck there either. We must regroup by discounting the negative thoughts over and over again. I had a very selfish mind-set, and now, I give to people without thinking about it. My prayer is, "God, today how can I bless someone?"

If you desire to be married, you must keep your finances in order. You can't mimic the same spending lifestyle in a new marriage covenant. Financial issues are high on the list for reasons for divorce in America.

> *"Now to Him who is able to do exceedingly*
> *abundantly above all we ask or think,*
> *according to the power that works in us..."*
> *Ephesians 3:20*

By spiritual experience and growth, God can restore your credit and allow you to become financially stable again. Just *trust* Him!

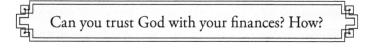
Can you trust God with your finances? How?

Personal Notes:

_____

_____

_____

_____

_____

_____

_____

_____

_____

_____

_____

_____

_____

_____

_____

_____

_____

_____

_____

_____

_____

_____

_____

_____
_____
_____
_____
_____
_____
_____
_____
_____
_____
_____
_____
_____
_____
_____
_____
_____
_____
_____
_____
_____
_____
_____

I will be proactive with my finances by
being mindful of what I spend and trusting
God to be a provision for my family!

CHAPTER 8

Totally Free in Christ

The world will tell us to throw in the towel and give up because our life does not seem to reflect "blessings."

> Why aren't you prospering? What's a pretty woman like you doing single? Oh, there must be something wrong with you.

Lies…

"Jesus turned and said to Peter, 'Get behind me, Satan! You are a stumbling block to me; you do not have in mind the concerns of God, but merely human concerns.'"
Matthew 16:23

I'm grateful that I didn't allow the devil's lies to consume me because of what people thought about me. Your goal is to please God, not man.

Being totally free in Christ is relying solely on God for every aspect of your life and being healed from an orphan spirit, unforgiving heart, fear, guilt, mistrust, rejection, gossip, loneliness, desperation, jealousy, anger, and a host of other ungodly characteristics and negative emotions.

We should be seeking God daily and spending quality time with Him. He should be our priority, and we will be judged by God if we don't. Be obedient to God's will for your life! Walking in obedience means walking in *victory*!

> *"For we must all appear before the judgment*
> *seat of Christ, so that each of us may receive*
> *what is due us for the things done while*
> *in the body, whether good or bad."*
> *2 Corinthians 5:10*

Are you totally free in Christ? If your answer is no, examine yourself immediately and ask God for guidance with clarity.

We make senseless excuses about why we can't serve God, but we can worship other things such as playing golf, attending football and basketball games, et cetera.

Sometimes we call on God's help only when we have a dire need due to a family or work crisis. We can't continue to use God as a backdrop when tough times arise. We must have Him in our hearts and at the forefront of our minds if we are having a good or bad day. Accept Him today and give your life over to Him and make certain you ask that His will be manifested in your life!

> What if God said, "You have no time for me, so now, I don't have any time for you"? What if God decided to turn His back on you?

I want God's hands on me at all times and I have a dire need for His presence daily in my life, not just during the challenging times either. When God decides to wake me up each morning, this is enough for me because I have one more day to get it right with my Father.

We allow the enemy to distract us with people and other pleasures. Satan's main goal is to take your focus off of God by derailing the divine plan for your life.

> Are you missing out on your blessings
> or prolonging your potential because
> of your disobedience to God?

The enemy has used everyone in my life to distract me. The greater your assignment, the greater the distraction. If God gives you an assignment, please follow through by seeking Him for guidance, wisdom, and understanding. Don't put God's assignment at the end of your list.

You're already equipped because God chose you to complete the assignment. Just be sensitive to His voice because He wants to use you to bless others who may be going through what you have already experienced. There is *power* in your purpose!

> I can't do this, God, so why are you
> asking me? Can you choose someone
> else to complete this project?

We continue to ask God questions that He already has the answers for, and we use people, jobs, or church as excuses not to obey God's will. God is tired of us complaining and not doing what He has called us to do for His kingdom. It's time to get serious with a sense of urgency!

My sister, I have been in this place many times, gripped with fear, thinking that no one would believe that I was called to serve in a higher capacity in ministry, but those who were close to me observed my soaring thirst for more of God and His Word.

At the time, I didn't have an abundance of biblical knowledge, and that kept me bound by the enemy! Satan had a grip on me with negative thoughts by continually telling me that I didn't have enough knowledge.

God has called all of us for a specific purpose, and we need to pray, fast, and ask for confirmation. I fasted for a great deal of time, and God continued to give me confirmation on how to serve in His kingdom. It's crucial that we seek our purpose on how we are called to serve God's people. Don't be afraid to allow God to use you, even with lack of knowledge of His Word.

When I prayed, *"God do a quick work in a short period of time in my life,"* I saw God's hand move quickly, but on His "timing," not mine.

I'm not speaking about praying for materialistic pleasures, but unconditional *love* toward others, joy, a discerning spirit, a kind spirit, et cetera. We must go to the throne of God with the right motives daily, again asking for His *wisdom*, guidance, clarity, power, understanding, strength, *peace*, and ultimate *joy*.

What have you been praying for lately?

"When you ask, you do not receive, because
you ask with wrong motives, that you may
spend what you get on your pleasures."
James 4:3

You must have a spiritual mentor and accountability partner because this is a key component of your growth. This person must be someone whom you can trust, a confidant, not the gossiping, needy friend. This person should be the praying friend who encourages you to do better and is deeply rooted in God's Word. This person should be willing to keep you on track and hold you accountable with love. God will use this person to deliver specific messages, instructions, or confirmation.

I relied heavily on the Reverend Todd Smith and evangelist Pearline Matson to assist me with the understanding of my calling. They supported me by interpreting my dreams and explaining Scriptures. When I had issues that caused me confusion or specific weaknesses, they were there for me. They guided me in managing my life with spiritual wisdom from God's Word. Their conversations affirmed what God had shared with me, and I received clarity. I am forever grateful for their love and gift of time.

> Do you have a spiritual mentor,
> accountability, or prayer partner?

Make certain that you ask God for permission because you will share confidential information, and your spiritual partner must be spiritual. They should pray for you without judgment and love you unconditionally as Christ loves them when they make mistakes.

As women, we all deal with the same struggles daily. Being a liberated woman of God means you can compliment another sister and be elated for her! But instead we focus on one flaw of the person, which is not having a loving, kind spirit.

We walk around with cluttered, broken spirits because we don't put on God's armor daily. We haven't let go of our past hurtful experiences, and, therefore, we are "damaged goods," but there is healing in Jesus Christ because He loves you so much and He has His best for you.

> Father God, I am ready to receive
> Your *best* for my life! I choose to put on
> the full armor of God daily!

"Finally, be strong in the Lord and in his mighty power. Put on the full armor of God, so that you can take your stand against the devil's schemes. For our struggle is not against flesh and blood, but against the rulers, against the authorities, against the powers of this dark world and against the spiritual forces of evil in the heavenly realms. Therefore put on the full armor of God, so that when the day of evil comes, you may be able to stand your ground, and after you have done everything, to stand. Stand firm then, with the belt of truth buckled around your waist, with the breastplate of righteousness in place, and with your feet fitted with the readiness that comes from the gospel of peace. In addition to all this, take up the shield of faith, with which you can extinguish all the flaming arrows of the evil one. Take the helmet of salvation and the sword of the Spirit, which is the word of God. And pray in the Spirit on all occasions with all kinds of prayers and requests. With this in mind, be alert and always keep on praying for all the Lord's people."
Ephesians 6:10–18

Have you ever been in a one-sided relationship? It does not feel good, does it?

God wants a mutual relationship with you. Allow God to shower you with His power and embrace His love for you! God will always love you.

I have been through many trials and tribulations, but through it all, I have spiritually grown and learned how to lean on and trust God for every aspect of my life. God allowed me to go through hurt after hurt for a reason.

At first, I was bitter and angry, but over time, I began to shift my thinking by realizing that my troubles were simply for my own good. As I mentioned earlier, Joseph endured so much hurt from his own family, but God had an ultimate plan and purpose for his life. It may have seemed bitter for Joseph in the beginning, but he had a sweeter deal in the end.

God can do the same thing for you, but He can't use us for His glory and we can't hear His voice unless we are healed of all of our past wounds and hurts. Make certain your spirit is free of cluttered thoughts and negative people. Discount the lies from the enemy and rebuke Satan immediately.

You must tell the devil that he has no authority over your life or your family's lives. We must pass our tests from God because He does allow certain situations to happen for "our good," as I mentioned earlier, just as Joseph exemplified in Genesis. Everything we do should be for the glory of God, even how we speak and approach others. The tongue is a powerful tool that can be utilized for blessing or cursing someone, especially our family.

Prayer:

> Lord, give us a hunger to hear and understand the truth of Your Word. Help us show Your love to others by faithfully living out its instructions for us. Amen.

Again, we must take up our cross and put on the whole armor of God daily. Your peace, joy, power, strength, well-being, stability, faith, marriage, relationships, children, and family are worth fighting for!

> *"When the devil steps to you, step up to him too, so fight, spiritually. . . Don't be a wimpy Christian when it comes to your faith; stand bold as a lion with confidence in Christ."*
> *Pastor Byron C. Stevenson,*
> *The Fort Bend Church*

We should approach God by being honest because He already knows our thoughts and situations before we ask Him to grant us anything. You can be real with God because He is always on a spiritual watch 24/7, interceding on your behalf.

As a daughter of the King, we should never have a defeated spirit because God has given you the necessary tools to combat the enemy. We must fight on our knees with prayer and watch God's manifestation in these areas of concern. You are blessed and highly, highly favored, so walk into your destiny and live on purpose for Christ. Focus on leaving a spiritual legacy for your children so that they will have a sense of urgency to serve God as they grow older.

You may have a busy schedule, but God should still be the focus of your life daily. He is the ruler of your life, the author and finisher of your faith. You don't have control over your life; God does.

How can you be free in Christ? What are the necessary steps you can put into action?

Personal Notes:

_____

_____

_____

_____

_____

_____

_____

_____
_____
_____
_____
_____
_____
_____
_____
_____
_____
_____
_____
_____
_____
_____
_____
_____
_____
_____
_____
_____
_____
_____
_____

I am totally free in Christ because He
has destined me for a purpose!

CHAPTER 9

Having Balance

As single parents, we must incorporate balance in our lives. We should allow time to enjoy a great view, take a trip, get a massage, spend time with girlfriends, exercise, or just have coffee at Starbucks alone. Time away from your children will allow you to regroup and return to them as a fruitful mom. Also, your children need a break from you as well, so it's a win-win situation.

God wants you to enjoy life, but keep Him first in everything that you do.

> *"After he had dismissed them, he went up*
> *on a mountainside by himself to pray. Later*
> *that night, he was there alone...."*
> *Matthew 14:23*

If Jesus needed time alone, we definitely require time alone as well. Don't think that you are a Superwoman who can do everything without breaks because this type of thinking is a runaway train that will eventually crash.

We must realize that it's okay to have some "me time" and not feel guilty about it. When you do have time away, don't call your children every five minutes, because worrying about them defeats the purpose of getting away.

If we don't take time alone, we can't be effective for our children or anyone else around us. You will know when your "I've had enough" attitude shows up, which means that you are overdue for a break.

> *"May God himself, the God of peace, sanctify*
> *you through and through. May your whole*
> *spirit, soul and body be kept blameless at*
> *the coming of our Lord Jesus Christ."*
> *1 Thessalonians 5:23*

The burnout syndrome normally shows up if we don't take time to rejuvenate our mind, body, and soul. At this point, we are no good for anyone, including ourselves.

Celebration is having a good time, but being ladylike too. Most men don't care to date loud, rude, disrespectful women, and they usually run from this type of behavior. Men are seeking a quiet spirited woman as the Bible tells us, a gentle, kind spirit.

*"Your beauty should not come from outward
adornment, such as elaborate hairstyles and
the wearing of gold jewelry or fine clothes.
Rather, it should be that of your inner self, the
unfading beauty of a gentle and quiet spirit,
which is of great worth in God's sight."*
1 Peter 3:3–4

Be mindful of how you portray yourself, especially in social settings. Please be aware of the fact that someone is always watching you. We are representing Christ when we go into the world, not ourselves.

We must juggle the following in our lives:

1) Serving in church
2) Children
3) Career
4) Family/friends
5) Dating (once healed)

All of the things listed above allow you to recognize that you need to manage your time wisely. Otherwise, you will be overwhelmed or emotionally unstable.

Don't waste your time with needy people who drain the life out of you, or relationships with men who are not going anywhere. Please be mindful of the usage of your time and be sensitively focused on what's important to God.

You must seek uncompromising peace by having a deep connection with God. God has told me not to answer the phone or call someone back because they were a distraction.

Having balance does not mean staying out all night or until the early morning hours either, but coming home at a respectable hour because your children are most likely waiting up for you. Just remember, your children are like sponges and they soak up everything that you do and say. Most importantly, they can sense and detect the truth. We must have high standards as the responsible adult and spiritual parent.

"...but set an example for the believers in speech,
in conduct, in love, in faith, and in purity."
1 Timothy 4:12

Another important aspect of balance is taking care of your body by eating healthy and exercising. I have been a power walker for many years now, and I love it. My body tells me when I need to go walking and this relieves my stressors.

Go online and do your research on how to be a healthier person. There is so much information on this subject that you can utilize.

Lastly, be cautious of the company that you keep, especially if they are not seeking God. It is very important to make certain that your lifestyle lines up with your character. The people you associate with are a reflection of you. Take inventory of your friends and start subtracting. When God closes one door and opens others, be thankful! God will add more friends later who are meant to be in your life.

> How can you have balance without being selfish? Do you love yourself enough to make the necessary changes? How does balance keep you from throwing in the towel?

Personal Notes:

_____

_____

_____

_____

_____

_____

_____

_____

_____

_____

_____

_____

_____

_____

_____

_____

_____

_____

_____

_____

_____

_____

_____

_____

_____

_____

_____

_____

_____

_____

_____

_____

_____

_____

*I have balance in my life, and I use my time
wisely by following what God desires for my life.*

CHAPTER 10

Learning to be Patient

J esus was very patient with His disciples. Sometimes they were lazy and wavered in their faith by focusing solely on themselves. They allowed doubt to creep into their minds by questioning who Jesus was as the Son of Man, and Jesus rebuked them with *love* when it was necessary.

I have struggled with being patient for many years, and my daughters can attest to that. I'm not sure why I haven't mastered it just yet. I have had periods when I have passed the test and times when I have failed miserably.

Whatever you desire for God to do in your life, He will provide it, especially if it is His will. Waiting for God to provide can be discomforting, but we must endure without complaining spirits so that we don't make hasty decisions that can deeply affect our families because we didn't receive permission from God. This leaves us regretful, and we still don't have what we truly desire.

Maybe you have walked away from God by not living righteously anymore because of your impatience, but remember that we can't trick or hide from God because He knows and sees everything.

God will meet all of your needs. He is aware and understands what you are going through during this season of your life and He still has your best interest at heart.

God commands you to obey and serve Him until He blesses you with what He has promised. Patience will give you a higher level of *faith* in Christ after our waiting period. Having faith means we are taking a risk. We don't have anything tangible, but as believers, we trust God. Now, once you receive your blessing, the long wait will disappear instantly from your mind, and the wait will be worth it!

> *"The LORD is good to those whose hope is in him, to the one who seeks him; it is good to wait quietly for the salvation of the LORD."*
> *Lamentations 3:25–26*

God allows trials to teach us valuable lessons. He's omniscient, meaning He's all-knowing and all-wise.

Impatient people are difficult to be around and to live with. It was difficult to be in my presence years ago because of my upbringing, but I slowly learned to change my attitude. We must correct our negative behavior while waiting.

Being patient is not a sign of weakness but of godly character. When someone is rude and you let it go, that means that you understand their shortcomings and you have a patient spirit. We can express to the person how they hurt our feelings in *love* because God's desire is not for people to treat us as doormats, mistreating us constantly by taking our kindness as a weakness.

> *"Brothers and sisters, as an example of patience in the face of suffering, take the prophets who spoke in the name of the Lord. As you know, we count as blessed those who have persevered. You have heard of Job's perseverance and have seen what the Lord finally brought about. The Lord is full of compassion and mercy."*
> *James 5:10–11*

God blesses those who persevere and wait patiently for Him to move in their situations, especially when others mistreat us. You should still treat others fairly and highly esteem them. With time, you will begin to implement this behavior in your life daily.

Don't judge or dismiss people for their faults because *grace* is looking for them and God shows them mercy daily as He does for us! God is still working it out for His good for them as well.

Are you easily frustrated? Why? How can you rely on God to assist you with your patience?

Personal Notes:

_____

_____

_____

_____

_____

_____

_____

_____

_____

_____

_____

_____

_____

_____

_____

_____
_____
_____
_____
_____
_____
_____
_____
_____
_____
_____
_____
_____
_____
_____
_____
_____
_____
_____
_____
_____
_____
_____
_____
_____

God has commanded me to be patient
in every situation in my life!

CHAPTER 11

Dating Plan as a Satisfied Single

D ating can be challenging as a single parent, and you must have a discerning spirit by listening to God's voice, which allows you to make wise decisions.

You must have a whole heart and be healed from your past wounds and hurts before you can love a man unconditionally. If you don't seek God and go through the healing process, unresolved emotions will resurface when you begin dating again, and that will be a disaster once the relationship has passed the new stage.

Being healed means that you are free from all of your past hurts and negative thoughts about your past relationship. This takes place when you acknowledge that you were mistreated as a child or an adult, but will not allow that to consume your life anymore because God has so much in store for your life. Therefore, you will not allow the devil to use a person or situation to deter God's plans because there is too much at stake for God's kingdom.

You must be content until God blesses you. Whatever it is that you desire in a mate, God still has ordained the perfect mate for you. He will be perfect in God's eyesight, not yours.

I dated someone for a while, but he proved to be wrong for me. However, he did teach me how to trust God, fast, and pray. My faith went to another level because of his faith in God. Everyone comes into our lives for a reason and a season, and every man whom you are attracted to is not meant to be a part of your journey.

When we try to assist God, it usually backfires. Whatever God is doing, it is not for you to understand, because it's spiritual, and when you operate with a carnal mind-set, you can't grasp spiritual understanding.

> *"Trust in the LORD with all your heart and
> lean not on your own understanding."*
> Proverbs 3:5

First, always set normal boundaries when dating—you are in control of your dating life. Be careful because our emotions can run wild with loneliness, fear, and rejection. With these mind-sets, we can't make wise decisions about dating. You must discount the devil when he makes you feel negative. You can't react on your feelings or negative emotions because that could block the man that God personally selected for you.

Secondly, the location you meet a man is very important. Places such as your church, the grocery store, friend/family gatherings, the gym, and a coffee shop are all great places to meet someone. Be cautious with social media, though. Be mindful of deceit, as godly people can conceal their true identities online. Dating still works by meeting someone in a public setting.

Thirdly, it's crucial that we date a godly man who has a fear of God's wrath, a deep personal relationship with God, and the reverence of Him in his life! This will allow your relationship to be fruitful and sustaining. When you are dating the wrong man, your spirit is vexed and this keeps you emotionally unstable. Many times, you don't realize it until you're away from the person, and then God reveals the truth when He has your complete attention.

Fourthly, pray for a high level of discernment daily. If a man can't commit to you without cheating and lying, then you are wasting your time because he is not complete in Christ. When he is not God-sent, you begin to work harder to overcompensate by spending your valuable time attempting to change him, but we can't change anyone. Only God can change someone's heart for the better.

So many times, God will show us deception and we ignore it because of our needy and lonely spirits. I have been in this same place, wanting to date someone because everyone around me was in relationships, but when you yield dating over to Christ, you're very clear and focused on His perfect plan and will, not your own plan. If it does not work out, it was not God's plan.

> *"For the word of God is alive and active. Sharper than any double-edged sword, it penetrates even to dividing soul and spirit, joints and marrow; it judges the thoughts and attitudes of the heart."*
> *Hebrews 4:12 KJV*

Dating becomes a distraction when it takes up your intimate time with God. There are only twenty-four hours in a day, and if you are wasting two hours of your time, it can make your journey stagnant.

> Utilize your time wisely and don't allow people who are not meant to be in your life to stay over their appointed time.

When God permanently removes someone from your life, don't rekindle the relationship out of guilt and not wanting to hurt their feelings. Instead, be sure that God is sending them back in your life. God may be trying to prevent you from grief. God has removed several people from my life, especially over the last seven years, and I have peace because the removal has kept me from additional heartache. This proves how much God loves me and He desires the best for me!

Lastly, you must adhere to the warnings that God gives you concerning dating. Sometimes, God tells us to walk away, but we don't always adhere to His voice. Listen to His small, still voice, and you won't make the same mistakes as you did in the past.

> God gives us a way to escape, but
> sometimes we are afraid to take the exit!

A red flag is a stop sign, telling us to stop and go the other way. Listen closely to the Holy Spirit. Use your spiritual discernment and pray without ceasing for the choices you make when dating. God knows what you need and when you need it. Please, learn to wait on His timing!

> What steps can you take to make sure you
> are listening to the Holy Spirit when God
> gives you permission to date again?

Personal Notes:

_____

_____

_____

_____

_____

_____

_____

_____

_____

_____

_____

_____

_____

_____

_____

_____

_____

_____

_____

_____

_____

_____

_____

_____

_____

_____

_____

_____
_____
_____
_____
_____
_____
_____
_____
_____
_____
_____
_____
_____
_____
_____
_____
_____
_____
_____
_____
_____
_____
_____
_____

I am not desperate for a mate, and I will
trust God with my dating plan!

CONCLUSION

have been through many difficult circumstances in my life, but they were used by God to bring out His best in me! I have allowed people to hurt and mistreat me over and over again, but if I had the chance to go back and change it, I would not change anything. My life has purpose and a divine calling for women who have been hurt deeply, such as myself.

At one point, I thought that God had forgotten me because of all of the hurt and pain I experienced from dating a few men who never had my best interest at heart, jealousy from fake friends, and certain family members who had bullying spirits toward me. Their actions were not the unconditional love that God shows me daily. God had to take me through the fire and He ordered my steps to set me up for *victory*, making me a better person.

My past has turned into having a solid faith foundation, peace, joy, and numerous blessings from many people, including strangers, and God gave me blessings that don't have a price tag attached to them. I am delivered from financial issues, anger, anxiety, an unforgiving spirit, keeping up with wrongdoings, feeling not good enough, caring what people think about me, and people looking at me differently because I am divorced. God has healed me for the better! I chose to change my mind-set and focus on things that mattered to Christ. I chose to walk in *victory* because God is the authority over my destiny!

When issues and forces attack me, I put my hope in Christ because there is always victory in Him. I no longer have to fret or be weary because God always has my best interest at heart.

I don't have a perfect life, but I am striving daily to be like Christ. I have decided to be content until God moves. My life is in God's hands, and He always knows what's best for me. No matter how I feel about someone or a situation, He is still in control.

When you release people back to God, that is when you become liberated with spiritual freedom! My hope is solely in Christ, and it took many unmet expectations and disappointments for me to arrive at this point. Now, I ask God to guard my mind and heart with His protected peace, knowledge, and understanding.

I've been through many storms, trials, and tribulations, but I am still here. I am unstoppable and unbreakable because I am the King's daughter! I am striving to leave a legacy for my daughters so that they can prayerfully impact others.

Don't allow people to keep you in bondage because of your mistakes and question who you are called to be by God. They are quick to judge you but never focus on themselves. They have an earthly mind-set by ignoring God's important business while focusing on being accepted by the world's standards.

I want to motivate you to be your best with Jesus's unconditional love and unmerited grace by trusting Him with every aspect of your life. His grace is sufficient for us, for our strength is made perfect in weakness. Most importantly, be obedient to God's will for your life.

At the end of the day, God still loves you! You're free through Christ because your debt was paid by Jesus on the cross two thousand years ago.

"But he said to me, 'My grace is sufficient for you, for my power is made perfect in weakness.' Therefore I will boast all the more gladly about my weaknesses, so that Christ's power may rest on me. That is why, for Christ's sake, I delight in weaknesses, in insults, in hardships, in persecutions, in difficulties. For when I am weak, then I am strong."
2 Corinthians 12:9–11

When you are not moved by your circumstances, this takes power away from the enemy! Ask God to heal you from spiraling negative emotions so that you can be a fruitful, loving, kind, and forgiving, mother, daughter, sister, aunt, friend, colleague, et cetera. You have the victory today! Walk into your destiny!

> *"And we know that in all things God works*
> *for the good of those who love him, who have*
> *been called according to his purpose."*
> Romans 8:28

What have you learned from reading
this book that has changed your life?

Personal Notes:

_____
_____
_____
_____
_____
_____
_____
_____
_____
_____

Trust God for every aspect of your life!

DAILY DECLARATIONS FOR VICTORY

1. I am more than a conqueror.

2. I matter to God daily.

3. My family is well-favored, and we receive God's abundant provision.

4. I am set free.

5. I give all of my worries and anxieties to you, God.

6. I am bold and confident.

7. I have the peace, joy, kindness, faithfulness, unconditional love, and self-control of God.

8. I have a heart like Christ, and I will grow and mature to walk in His ways.

9. I am fearfully and wonderfully made by you, God.

10. I forgive all who have wronged me in the past.

11. My family is covered by the blood of Jesus.

12. I have divine healing for my mind, emotions, and will.

13. Seal me with Your peace, character, and spirit, God.

14. I'm blessed coming in and going out.

15. I can do all things through Christ who strengthens me.

16. God has not given me a spirit of fear. He gives me power, love, and self-discipline.

17. I meditate on God's Word day and night.

18. I am blessed in the city and blessed in the field.

19. The Lord makes me the head and not the tail, above only and never beneath.

20. My ways please the Lord, and He makes my enemies be at peace with me.

21. The joy of the Lord is my strength.

22. I am steadfast in my mind. He keeps me in perfect peace because I trust Him.

23. I am anxious for nothing.

24. The Lord has chosen me as His special treasure.

25. God forgives all my iniquities and heals all of my diseases.

26. I have a wholesome tongue, which is a tree of life to myself and others.

27. My prayers are powerful and effective.

28. I am dead to sin and alive to obeying God.

29. I prosper in all of my relationships.

30. God supplies all of my basic needs.

31. I am redeemed from the hand of the enemy.

32. I am an heir to the blessings of Abraham.

33. I walk by faith and not by sight.

34. I am destined for greatness.

35. I am a blessing to many wherever I go.

36. I am free from bondage and strongholds.

37. I have favor, grace, and new mercies today.

38. Do a quick work in a short period of time in my life for Your glory, God.

39. My business is prospering.

40. God, you have a powerful plan for my life.

41. My children will be a blessing to many.

42. My children will serve you, God, with gladness.

43. Allow me to love without judging.

44. Give me a kingdom mind-set.

45. Let me show others grace when they fail.

46. I have the fruit of the Spirit daily.

47. God is in control, not me.

48. The Lord is my shepherd, I shall not want or lack any good thing.

49. I surrender to Your will, God.

50. I desire to be closer to God daily because I am leaving a legacy for my children.

Speak God's blessings and
promises over your life daily!

ABOUT THE AUTHOR

Desolyn Hicks is a speaker, minister, biblical counselor, and mentor. She has received training from the Inspire Women Leadership Academy; serving as a participant and facilitator for Inner Circles. She holds a Bachelor's in Business Management from Letourneau University and a Bachelor's of Biblical Counseling from the College of Biblical Studies.

Desolyn has been afforded many opportunities to share her story of divorce recovery, single parenthood, overcoming cultural stigmas, and financial hardships. Her life is truly an example of God's amazing grace.

She is blessed to be the proud mom of two beautiful daughters.